PRAISE FOR

Stemming the Flow is un
Ducker is a close observer
what exists outside of hims
of witty light verse, passio ..... on aging,
books, music, the natural world and more, he is therefore far better
than most poets at evoking the dramatic dimensions of our lives.
Unlike most novelists who turn to verse, Ducker knows his versecraft
cold and gives us well-turned lines in both meter and free verse
throughout. American poetry needs more work like this, which is so
measured and meaningful that it brings everything it touches, even
death, into harmonious relationship, thereby transforming mere
experience into an intense, focused linguistic encounter with the
world. This is the kind of writing that deserves the name 'poetry.'

David Rothman author of six books of poetry and
Unlocking the Secrets of English Verse

From deeply poignant poems about the loss of a spouse to a
brilliant retelling of the fall of Ikaros, from playful poems about
scarecrows and Smith-Coronas to a sonnet on Bach, Bruce
Ducker brings a wealth of erudition, formal skill, and sparkling
wit to a remarkable range of subjects. Readers disenchanted
with the aridities of postmodernism will find much to remind
them of the essential pleasures of poetry in Stemming the Flow.

John Brehm, author of *No Day at the Beach* and *Dharma Talk*;
winner of the Brittingham Prize

I like your poems... I'm amazed by your rhyming. So few people
these days attempt formal poems. 'Dappled' is my favorite [and]
'Willy Loman' is fun.

Donald Hall, U. S. Poet Laureate, 2006-2008;
Winner, National Medal of Honor

STEMMING THE FLOW

POEMS

BOOKS BY BRUCE DUCKER

Novels

Dizzying Heights

Mooney in Flight

Bloodlines

Lead Us not into Penn Station

Marital Assets

Bankroll

Failure at the Mission Trust

Rule by Proxy

Short Story Collection

Home Pool: Stories of Fly-fishing and Lesser Passions

Poetry

Stemming the Flow

STEMMING THE FLOW

POEMS

Bruce Ducker

KU
PRESS

A catalogue of this book is available from the British Library

ISBN 978 1 909 36278 9

Typeset in Bodoni 72

Editorial and Design by Kingston University
MA Publishing Students: Rachel Matthews, Annie Monge,
Kirsten Oshodi-Glover, and Katie Pierce

First Published in Great Britain 2024
KINGSTON UNIVERSITY PRESS
Kingston University
Penrhyn Road,
Kingston-upon-Thames

KT1 2EE

Acknowledgments

My thanks to these journals and their editors; to Emma and the Emmanators at Kingston University Press; to the readers Sue Bickert, John Brehm, Alan Danson, Josiah Hatch, and Bruce Smith; to the poet Mark Scott for tutelage and editing; and for all this and more, with love to Mary G. McGrath.

Many of these poems first appeared elsewhere:

"After Run-off," Gray's Sporting Journal
"At the Foot of Maroon Bells," The Quarterly
"The Barge," Southern Review
"Coyote," Crosswinds
"The Cricket in the City," Poetry Magazine
"Fragment," Commonweal
"The Frying Pan in Winter," Commonweal
"Gershwin Visits," Press
"Idlock," The Partisan Review (retitled)
"I Guess Your Dreams," New York Quarterly (retitled),
"Intaglio," Cedar Press Review (revised)
"Lines in Elegy," The Human Touch (U. of Colorado)
"Love at the Diner," Ascent Review
"Making a Poet," The Quarterly (retitled)
"My Brother and Schrödinger's Cat," Last Stanza
"On Monster.com," Crosswinds (revised)
"Pantomime Horse," Crosswinds
"Picnic," Poetry Magazine
"Prairie Gossip," The Quarterly
"Shades," Partisan Review
"The Monitor," Last Stanza
"Time, Rate, Distance," The Wallace Stevens Journal
"To an Old Man Dying," The New Republic
"Waiting for Life," The Literary Review (retitled)
"Zodiac," Comstock Review

Contents

Beginnings

Places in the World

Love and Marriage

Death and Dying

Making Art

Beginnings

It sometimes seems as if...
--Robert Frost (when asked to define poetry)

My poems must stand on their own,
the legless little cripples.
—Dylan Thomas

Making a Poet

Remember when you knocked your mother's
Crystal tortoise from the end table?
Not meaning to. You spun to outdraw the mirror
And caught the weight full with an elbow,
Parked, as it was, too close to the edge.
Density itself sailed to the floor,
Shattering on the threshold into splinters.

Wouldn't you know the damn thing would
Miss the carpet, otherwise wall
To wall, and explode into razor eggs.
Now in a distant city, on the floor
Of your own house, you rest your hand.
A dot of glass pricks your thumb,
And you can hardly stem the flow.

My Brother and Schrödinger's Cat

When my brother died (perhaps now,
Perhaps some time from now,
Say, twelve or fifteen years hence),
I got to thinking. While we weren't close,
We shared a room. He taught me hockey,
And jazz, the Brunswick label, Blue Note,
The off-beat, the flatted fifth, double-time,
Kook, Diz, Chet. Desmond's alto runs
Through my life, my Ariadne's thread.

His radio played from midnight on.
I'd awake to showers of notes, flooding down
Like starfall, listen awhile, fall back asleep.
When he played his clarinet, it squealed
As if being strangled. He'd put on a disc
And struggle to comp behind the soloist.
Chase him up and down the scale,
Landing on the note every so often, the way,
In traffic, sometimes you see the same car.

His horn was weak, but his whistling
(He did a great rendition of Salt Peanuts)
Would have won him first chair in any band,
Kenton, Basie, Mingus, Duke. If only
They scored charts for a whistler.

I got to missing him, especially during
Stanley Cup finals, so I went to visit him
In Pasadena, and he still whistles great.

Teens

The tanager chick was
Next to fledge,
But his mother would not
Let him leave unless he changed
Into something suitable.

Gershwin Visits

1.
One hundred glass pianos
Connected by ladders.
Among the rungs my father hangs,
Humming those tunes.

2.
Ivory cigarette holder
Clenched at a presidential angle.
Smoke, a tenor line,
Floats through the fretted grill.

3.
From his height my father nails a talisman
To each doorpost.
Jessel, Benny, the bat of Hank Greenberg,
The mash of those crushing harmonies.
And where he was seen—
Chasen's, the Brown Derby. Best of all,
Himself
Captured by the Pathé camera,
A day on the beach with Harpo.

4.
Foot-high swells of Rhapsody in Blue, surfing clarinet.
Not the New Land discovered
But the plate tectonics that
Move the island under him, aligned in the Hudson
Pointing north like a needle.

5.

Notes nail a trellis.

Notes soldered to staff, thirteenths

Dropped in the street, sharped ninths

Stuck on the Williamsburg Bridge where they

Could flatten a tire. Look at that, will you?

Somebody must have spilled them off the back

Of a truck.

6.

When he spoke over the surf,

What did Harpo say?

7.

My father humming the tunes,

Shot by his roadster, tan upholstery, glissands

Across the wire-strung bridge to the Riviera.

The Riviera burns down, Oscar Levant dies smoking

His sponsor's product.

Photographs

Slip loose from the heavy black page.

8.

Score for Klezmer horns and drums,

Drum heads white and starched,

Boiled shirt fronts, licorice sticks,

Keyboards from slides in the parks,

From chained swings down slides and up ladders.

9.

His fingers sit the keys,
Tent the keys, twelve fingers
Sit the see saw of his chords, monochromatic
Sequence, black on white rotogravure.
Wont you tell him please to put on some speed,
Follow my lead
My mother sings over the linen's fold, wet
Perfume of ironing and wood,
Watching over me, over me
A brown gravy covers me, carrot
And brisket alike. Sweet scent on the wind,
Gravy steam rising.

10.

In newsreels he and Harpo wear striped robes.
My father wears white.
Scallop-edged prints fit neatly in triangular pockets
That we have glued to the page.
The glue is drying.

11.

The youth of them all rises,
A cloud over a warm island.
Distant and gradually moving at us,
Blowing at us, full of the chill rain of time.

The Monitor

Dimmed by time,
The boys compete to earn freedom:
Raising the flag, guarding the crosswalk,
Filling ink into shot-glass wells.
None so covert as blackboard monitor.
Even in seedling days I find
Shadowy solace in soliloquy.

I collect the day's erasers,
Bulging my canvas shoulder bag,
Tote them to the fenced yard.
Walls stilled of hand-ballers,
Yard stilled of spud, stick-ball, fungo,
The felts clapped on masonry brick
Breathe Aladdin puffs of dialog balloons.

A jinn of images as
Motes assemble, filings to a magnet.
Lessons: loops of Palmer Method,
Lie and lay conjugated with sniggers,
Quotients stranded on the roofs of their huts.
A diagrammed sentence, clauses akimbo,
Branches like a locust across the blackboard.

Years later, at the Spring Street station,
I spot that locust on a subway map,
And catch the unshakable whiff of chalk.

Letdown

Youth is disappointed in the past.
It's hazy and incorporeal,
Reception cloudy, subtitles fast,
A nag, a scold, a required tutorial.

He finds the future plays another flop,
Distant, unreliable, opaque,
Iffy beyond use, no curtain, non-stop--
Either bromidic or incredible, fake.

So what's his opinion on the present?
Real-time action, reality blasts,
Here today, tactile and pleasant--
But, the down-side, it never lasts.

Gridlock

We're late.
In the cross-street a reticulated bus
The size of Kansas stands,
Immensely perpendicular,
Its indifference unparticular,
Ignoring our demands,
Ignoring traffic, stasis, us,
Our fate.

What's worse,
Every cycle of the signal gets extended.
The green glows for an entire day,
And no one moves. The red glares all night,
Saint Jude a faint, irrelevant light,
And we wait, a diabolical delay,
Wondering how and whom we've offended,
Our curse.

Tin Soldier

I have a friend who enjoys
Commanding his vanities and ambitions
To war with his instincts for charity.
And, more, enjoys watching his comrades
Fret for the noble, human side.
We both recognize the resemblance:
The little boy who assembles his soldiers,
Facing each other, equalizing the lines,
Knowing all the while which side will win.

Revelation

I remember my mother, my father too,
saying more often than once, Someday you'll understand,

And I have this vision.
A magenta sky, the clouds drawn
by Banksy –he's way up on the scaffold–
Stairs by Busby Berkeley, the wall (no pearly gates,
the ads are bullshit) just a wall over which we float.
Now a long row of slums. "This is the arts district,"
My guide goes, "You'll be housed here. Used to be
factories." The streets full of souls–at one café there's
Bird and Bach, scatting, Bird's Conn in his lap,
Except when he picks it up, licks the reed, and blows a
line that screams down the alleys, you could hang clothes on it.
My guide tells or reminds me (now there's no
difference) we've met before, but I swear she must be
two hundred years old, and I get queasy, maybe
Chiles rellenos, wondering what could have happened,
'cause she's wearing this smirk. And, am I glad, a lot else.
Anyway we get to the end of the block,
turn the corner, and she goes, "You got lucky,
top floor corner. Great view." And she points east
to where a city gleams gold as the alto, the way
you'd expect, and I go, "So why do I get this? It looks
like the dump I lived in when I was a kid," and she goes,
"Someday you'll understand,"
And honest to God,
I don't.

Ikaros

Whose fault was it? Do not blame
A sun that innocently rolled its rails,
Oblivious to trivial traffic below.
No malice there, thousands of H-bombs
Firing each minute and a schedule to keep.
Do not blame the air that supported him,
Nor the sea that swallowed him. Him,
His feathers, the wax, the work, the youth.

The trouble starts with the owner.
Any tradesman will tell you that.
The owner imprisoned us to build a palace
For his queen, who used a wooden bull
For pleasure.

Sex is always there, isn't it?
A labyrinth to hide the hideous offspring.
The boy and I, jailed to do his bid.
A tower, a thousand gulls our neighbors.

Querulous gulls asking, Why not leave?
The answer: the surrounding sea.
I am, after all, a craftsman. When there are problems,
They are mine to solve. Materials, design,
And always the physics. The numbers were mine,

You cannot blame the boy.
I called him Magpie, a name he liked.
His first task, the theft of royal hives

At night, softly stealing sleeping bees,
Drowning them in tide pools, yes a murder,
Insecticide, I joked, but he gathered the wax.
And scrounged parchment, wood.
I taught him honest knots to braid the rawhide.
Should I not?

Feathers their own science: coverts, seconds.
Odd that they call it down, for it lends
Warmth and lift.

Lift!
Of drag and thrust, lift and weight,
Lift our god. On corvid wing, the boy stole,
Cajoled and traded. I studied gulls,
Their ratios: surface to weight, wing loads.
With grain we trapped stray pigeons
Not wishing to dissect our neighborly peers.
Should I have disregarded the physics?
I, who built automatons for children of royals,
Now animated a wing. Joints, membranes, controls,
What shape an edge to part the air?
Tests on moonless nights, on tower roof:
Angle of attack, yaw control, crab and slip.
The boy held aloft the aerofoil, cunningly wrought,
While I instructed, heard his trapped-vole squeals

As wind inched his sandals from the tiles.
Should I have said No? no joy, no pleasure?

Should I have not taught him the sciences?
And all the while importunate gulls.
Grounded by theory and speculation.
The horizontal component of lift,
Oscillations that shivered his body.
The boy was eager, but never reckless.
I encouraged him. Be bold, Magpie, be brave.
He would respond with Athenian learning.

I shook him by the shoulders. Nothing in Excess?
Moderation? Those words chain us to earth.
But Father, what of the Golden Mean?
Followers of the Golden Mean eat
Grass soup and biscuits. Easy to lure the young.
The boy flew as the hawk fledges.
Be bold, Magpie. Follow me.

Bold: that flesh-in-throat leap from the nest.
The gulp of free-fall when life leaks through
Body openings, the eyes, the anus,
Until invisible zephyrs catch him, buoy him.
Once up, I could not keep him down. Rolls, first,
Full stalls off the ground, landings low and hot,
Loops, chandelles envied by the swallows.
Dutch rolls that maintain the heading.
One night, envious, an owl tracked him home.
The day of departure, I was the student,
And timid at that. I, who had raised

Woodcraft to science, would now raise man.
I warned, Too low, we're lost in mist,
Too high we insult the gods.
His eyes were on the dawn, ablaze.
Was I to quit? I saw first light

In those eyes, bent and kissed his mouth.
A plover feeds its chicks mouth
To mouth and I fed him death.
The end you know. If fault were found,
Would it firm the wax? Once I called out.
As wax watered and the first barbules
Broke free, molted, snow flakes
Returning my kiss, I called out.
Grass soup, he hailed back, and stepped
Into the void, Father. Follow me.
I buried his body in the Sienna sands
Of a stingy island, and traveled on,
Dragging the frame all the way to Syracuse.
I'll replace broken struts, the feathers it lacks,
Secure the knots, a needless landing or two,
And one dawn, follow him. Take wing.

Look, Ma

Remember that hammered brass letter opener,
Souvenir of your European trip?
When I get a new book of poems,
I use that to hold the pages,
And read them while I lunch
So my hands are free
To grip the sandwich,
And I sound out each letter,
The way you taught me.

Place in the World

Una piedra en el camino
Me enseñó que mi destino
Era rodar y rodar
Rodar y rodar, Rodar y rodar
— José Alfredo Jiménez.

Few people have the imagination for reality.
— Goethe

Out beyond ideas of wrongdoing and rightdoing
there is a field. I will meet you there.
— Rumi

The Cricket in the City

The cricket in the city saws his single call
Unremitting, unremitted, ignored
It prospers in silence, fills the night's hall
Fills the ear of the deaf and bored
Fakes the absence of a living thing
Then fades under the taxi horn
Below the radio's pop and the light
Of the blue television porn
And the cursing of the driver to come out and fight
Unheard for the drone of engine and fan,
Far below the reach of the phone's ring
Sinking further still from the grasp of the man
Who sits in the window of his hotel room,
Searching the blank street for thoughts to utter,
Smoking a last cigarette in the gathering gloom
And flicking the butt into the gutter.
Its ashes splash in spindrift spark, then die
Out, no drama, no love, no pity
No wings no chance to fly,
Like the cricket in the city.

Traveling the Southwest

In Wray Colorado a taxi driver, Wray's only,
Whose wife leads calisthenics at the senior center,
Teaches crafts, papier-mâché, helps to knit
Coasters and God's Eyes, leads songs,
Parks by the airstrip in his '96 Pontiac Firebird.
He watches for a plane to land, waits for a call. Mostly
He sits at the counter –Ming's Garden Chinese– and
Talks with Gladys over a Thor's cup of coffee. Sundays,
If you need a ride, you'll wait until after
Invitation, benediction, and postlude.

In Huachuca Arizona the arroyo that fringes
The San Pedro is often dry. Grey cottonwoods
Grow there, and rabbit brush, not much else.
Each spring tanagers, color of fire-coal,
Flit the riverbank, and are
Seen only by the barber, who with no trade
Comes here to eat his lunch from a bag.

In Rodeo New Mexico, not far from the border, the owner
Of the art gallery, when she was young and graceful,
Modeled for a sculptor who cast her buttocks in Lucite.
The work now hangs on her wall, clad in
Tight denim shorts. Annie's Ass, the locals call it.
These towns with neither hope nor despair
Simply stand, and the people in them trust that way,
Trust that their town will grow to be like them
And, more, they like it.

Prairie Gossip

Have you ever been out four counties east,
Where the wind dresses in dust and the threshers
Dance the milk dance and a magpie is mayor?
I went once. Drove through summer to sip iced tea
And watched through the diner's bruised glass.
Five-axles from Scottsbluff to Goodland
Came together for a bath and a square meal,
Pulled up their capes for an old-fashioned chat.

October on the Père Marquette

Sunk dark in the freshening water,
Water black as it is green,
The color of oak and bark,
Steelhead lie in formation, wagging
Windsocks alert in a breeze,
To feed on roe of salmon.
In a downpour, they have swum upstream
Lured by an encrypted scent
Of spawning hens and new rain.

On Monster.com

I was cruising the web when my eye stuck on the ad.
I'd been window-shopping, résumés and jobs, but
The screen ended my search.

BE A CLOUD? NO EXPERIENCE NEEDED

MUST ENJOY TRAVEL AND THE OUTDOORS.

NO BROKERS OR ACROPHOBES

I interviewed and was hired, I guess for my sincerity.
When I asked for the monster, they said, You'll see.
Probation went without a hitch. Mostly gliding,
Drifting, scudding. Weather formations. The perils
Of condensation. After ground school, I was sent aloft.
Early assignments were easy, cyclonic, counter-cyclonic.

In this line, one's career soon forks:
Stratus—the pea soup legion—or cirrus,
Suspended and crystalline. The blue skies, the chance to soar.
The cottony stuff that one associates with balmy days,
Polonius, green hill-sides. That was for me: I found my calling.
On the lookout for lovers lying in shade, they watching for me,
I puffed myself into a whale, replete with spindrift spout.
She pointed me out, nudging him from a doze
On her lap, to view me. He dreaming of building her a castle
Of song. And as he rose on an elbow, shading his eyes
With poems he had brought to read her, I morphed
Into a dragon, virga streaming from fleecy nostrils.

My first anniversary review was quite positive,
Accompanied by a substantial raise.

Flying to Bozeman

Is there evidence of life?
Scrub oak trace arroyo beds in dull yellow wool,
A child's sewing card. The marl nap
Blanched by early sands of snow,
Dakota lime chalks the back sides of buttes.
Steel machines comb dry furrows and
A mechanical irrigation wheel buries dimes in the dust.
Is there life? Look to the rivers that blade the land,
The Big Horn and Chugwater, Clark's Fork, the Tongue.
The Encampment, a flat miracle
Chromed by the high sun. That metal blankets
Stippled fish moving to spawn, that metal
And not the dull geometry of town,
Signals of survivors.

Intaglio

The peach conceals its ambiguities
In its pit, a map of dimensions.
More than scored, the flesh is revealed
Scarlet from the stone's wall.
Take note of that coronal rose
Seeped into its swaddle through,
We discover by devouring it
All that the peach knew.

Franconia Notch

When at last the Old Man leapt, brodied—
An insult to the legend of things granitic—
It was neither kidneys, nor cancer,
Nor any of the maladies humans undergo.
Nor felo-de-se caused by pains arthritic,
Nor by a life of solitude, internal, monastic,
Nor a longing for life's pastries sybaritic;
Nor the angst of questions without answer.
No, he simply tired of
Watching the blunders below.

Walt Whitman in Gehinnom

I adopt each theory, myth, god, and demi-god....

Have you noticed, he asks with a wink,
How Nature deals with ownership
Without a moment's debate of capital,
Collectivism, legacy?
Thunderstorms belong equally
And eternally to us all,
Indivisible and vested,
As does the sea's spindrift,
Wind through fields of rye.
Clouds of gnats, of ice;
Bramble and poppy,
Influenza and the croup,
Abscission and allelopathy,
Nakedness and attraction,
And indeed desiccation and death.
Even we, fixed in amplitude
And excess, might benefit
From close observation.

Hermeneutics

Visitors from Alpha Centauri have arrived.
They parked above the radar,
Below the eye of the Webb.
Consistent with protocol,
They reached us through our poets.
By hacking our computers, they
Deciphered our language,
Even words –jealousy, greed, cruelty–
For which they have no equivalent.

We're stuck, they write. Tell us
Why each of you treasures senseless words,
Eight runes or more, that include
Upper and lower cases, numbers and
One special character.

Mass at Velocity

When he conceived the touchstone theory,
Einstein, a mere youth
Of thirty-five, stood against the speed of light
As absolute truth.

He curved the universe, amending the work
Of the Second Day,
And caromed spheres of equivalence
Off relativity and into play.

But he neglected his years in time-space. His age was
Happily convenient.
If only he'd had the thought after sixty, he might have
Been more lenient.

Why the speed of light? Not, say, that of a gazelle,
An eland, a rabbit?
At age energy dissipates, not so much
Force as habit.

As I move through time my clock
Lingers at every loss
Now my mass walks, does not run, and slows
Where children cross.

Time x Rate x Distance

The problems posed are incomplete.
If Henry rides his bike to Pearl's,
Six miles away, what rate will assure
He arrives before Pearl departs?
Unknown to Henry, Pearl leaves her home
At noon and walks four miles per hour,
Stops a friend for a five-minute chat,
And reaches the yarn store at half-past one.
How far in all has she traveled?

No word of Henry's purpose? Blocked
By the faint sweat on his brow?
What is Pearl planning to knit?
Will a tie match Henry's colors?
We do not fret Pearl's endurance,
But what to think of the cryptic friend?

And other riddles crouch within.
What Time into Distance yields languor?
Life at what Rate equals anxiety?
Science measures only surfaces.
Solve for Henry, solve for Pearl.

Cedar Waxwing

For its weight, the word barbule
(the wisp at the end of a bird's feather)
packs more punch than any other.
I was floored to discover two,
shed by the feeder,
one with the red of passion, the other
tipped yellow as joy itself.

The Frying Pan in Winter

Its hundred pools curl over boulders
The size of cars. Amid the rock, speckle-back
Trout move easily in the summer of my mind,
Rising to the hatch, sipping lazily
Among thick-bodied bits of shrimp,
Ephemerellid nymph. Now that it is winter,
The green water tunnels through glass hoods.
Snow has sharpened the crack
Of gravel and the long, skewered light
Lantern-beams briefly on the moonscape bed.
Now that it is winter, no one wades
The Seven Castles' pool and upstream a single
Fisherman gently unhooks his prey
And slips it back like a book to the shelf.
Clamps his hand under the armpit. It is an easy
Day of short sun, and the dense water
Verging to ice warms only
The oxbows of memory.

After Run-off

A moment comes when the mud
That conceals sculpin, trout,
The mottled pebbles of the bed,
Long suspended, settles out.

Now shine through pocket suns,
Each star without a planet,
A ribbon of silky way,
Copper, pyrite, granite.

Each light its own construct
An energy in every clast,
Chips that mock gemstones,
Amber baked and glassed.

In that moment clouds are flushed,
Revealing what all clouds know–
The flood abates, and so June gives way
To summer's clear, abiding flow.

Winterscape

Snow on headstones
In the old cemetery:
Frosting on pound cake,
Nature redundant.

Coyote

Slips there the lone coyote
Gray as the arid cliff he climbs,
Dry and dusty and living on hunger.
The Navajo say he brought death
Into the world, others say he stole
Light from the spirits and left it,
Rotting, on our doorstep, to divine
Its use.

Cousin to the wolf, they are
Enemies, competitors. Even myth
Is not his friend. He is best known
For howling at the darkness,
His protest against solitude.
On the flats, his answer is the wind.
But in the high mountains, he succeeds
In making, not an ally,
But an echo.

Love and Marriage

A happy marriage is a long conversation
which always seems too short.
— André Maurois

Men and women, women and men.
It will never work.
-Erica Jong

Love at the Diner

Let me be the bacon
To your tomato heart.
Heavy on the mayo, light
On the toast. Deal the lettuce
Leaves from their round deck.
Tear the ends
Of paper straws and launch
Their sheaths into the far
Stratosphere, booths beyond,
Our foreheads touching over
Vanilla cokes as we sip.

First Sight

Disembarking from the train,
The lady and the gent
Caught each other's eye
And, much later, the rest.

At the Foot of Maroon Bells

It takes a particular light
That must be mixed to prescription.
To start, the haymeadow sun is boiled
By first frosts, then
Swirled in the mortar of
A mountain sky, crushed
By the pestle of igneous rock
And forced through a colander of
Leaves soft and gold as skin.
That light, properly bent,
Shaded from the eye by a
Lover's salute, refracted
And held steady, can dazzle, stun
Time on his march. Halted
Until the sunspot fades, he
May let us lie here a moment longer.

Dappled

They sat in the new sun that stolen morning,
She in a nightdress with lace neckline.
And when they went back to bed,
Found that the sun had stenciled
A spray of stars on her chest.
They are no longer, he, she,
The nightdress, the freckles.
Where are they?
Time and Night, chiastic hands washing,
Have washed them away,
But to where?

Edna and Eve

Nights he dreamed of Eve,
Too, when he drank bourbon
Or played his guitar.
Edna watched his dreams on the ceiling,
And threw him out.
Now he lives with Eve
And when he sings, dreams
Of Edna.

Goodbye Herring

Goodbye herring
Goodbye Joan
Goodbye loving
Pant and moan

Ciao endeavor
Shalom care
Well, whatever,
Bull and bear

Condiments of sin
Liver and bacon,
Vermouth and gin
Silverly shaken.

Cigarettes
Chances missed
Stacked regrets
All unkissed.

Death's a mess,
Seeds unsown,
But I confess
I'll miss Joan.

Tiles

"Exactly my story," she said
As they lay staring at a ceiling
Of tiles, acoustical, identical.
"I've gone from partner to partner,
Looking for fidelity."

Mirrors

In Mirrours, there is the like Angle of Incidence,
from the Object to the Glasse, and from the Glasse
to the Eye. —Francis Bacon, Novum Organum

How is it that these angles corroborate,
Cooperate, to arrive at the glass
And depart, reflect as a perfect match?
Geometry is admired for its chasm from our lives,
We marvel at theorems and proofs immune
From jealousy, appetite, remorse.

Sir Francis describes not simply the mirror
But the mechanics of marriage, and thus life.
When the angle of reflection is greater
Than the critical angle, all light enjoys reflection.
If p then q. If it rains, then
They cancel school. If they cancel school,
Then it rains. If it does not rain, then
They do not cancel school. Thus life is described
Not by inverse and converse, but
By contrapositives. Thus we live, we love;
We don't live, we don't love; and we die.

Picnic

They put away the plates and lay
In the eye of the sun. He locked her words
In the rocks and whispers in the pine needles.
They pressed their bodies into the ground
And in the shallows spread secrets.
Her cries of joy she hid in the chalcedony,
Sank them in the quartz rivers of outcrop.

Next spring, when the earth shifted,
The cries slid out, and jays and juncos
Rallied to see what was the ruckus.

Insight

Talking, she explained with care,
Takes two to play, not one.
But talking, as I'm well aware,
Is easier said than done.

I Guess Your Dreams

I watch you sleep.
Actors whose names I do not know appear on stage.
Someone is there.
He pinches your brow,
Pushes the clay together with finger and thumb
And with the point of an orange stick,
Scores a line by the bridge of your nose.
He leaves.
A landscape slides down your eyelids
Breathes out your nostrils the
Hay tickles your lips into a smile
And the hills fall upon your breast.
I walk among them.
An electron speeds across the footlights
Announcing a scene change.
You stir.

Premonitions

Why, she wonders, must dreams disappear?
Their faerie lenses cloud in first light
And with them the reason, besides fear,
We hold each other in the fleeting night.

Why build them of such dewy stuff
That leaves no hint or print on the mind,
Merely a ghost of feeling, not enough
To link, couple, match, or bind?

From bed's far borders each now stirs,
Seeks the string on dream's balloon.
Can't they tangle, his and hers?
Perhaps tonight, drawn by a different moon,

My dream and his, call and response,
A jigsaw of ovals, lacking lock or key,
What I fear and what he wants:
Compound subjects need a verb to agree.

If Tears Were Red

What if tears were red,
And stained the face, a cedar sap
Ageing to amber, cooling to solid:
Each of us human, each of us branded?

What if misdeeds weighed on our backs,
Heavy as mercury, forcing joints to snap,
Crippling us cringing squatters, crooked
On the sidewalks, alone, stranded?

What if flesh were clear,
Bones opaque, heart bared—not a sump flap,
But the pouch where love and pain lie hid—

Uncloaking pity, passion revealed, candid?

Lovers and Rubies

I

Rubies form in a furnace fired
By the collision of continents.
Rock folds under rock in ferocious heat,
Transmuted, crystalline. Atoms
Reshuffle to allow light to pass.
Corundum aligns into a lattice, colorless
Save where trace elements, impurities,
Rare rogue ions of chromium,
Distort, diffract, trap blue light,
And reflect back red.
Cosmologists note these goings-on
In algebraic formulae
That take some counting.

II

Slides his white wrist down her breast.
The prominent nub,
Memento vitae, suggests more.
There follow palm and fingers
Until the arm has fed its fill.
His lower lip is next to sip,
Too its vermillion border
And the skin, the slick skin below,
That covers the muscle
Orbicularis oris, that moves the mouth,
Skin he has taken care to shave close
So its lubricity might match hers.

III

13 million light years away,
Visible to these lovers, were they watching,
Two neutron stars coincide, explode.
No diamond in sunlight, but a thousand suns squared
In the flash of a brilliant-cut jot of hydrogen.
First, the ripples of space-time. Seconds later,
A spurt of gamma rays that glows blue and,
As it spends itself, a lapidary red.

All expected. The physicists, the cosmologists,
The astronomers knew it was coming to the second.
(They named the galaxy, NGC 43,
In iambic dimeter,
Common in nursery rhymes—
The clock struck one).

IV

Spent from their stab at completion,
They lie still, he the letter I at rest
In the cradle she forms for him.
They wait for dusk to make love again,
Indeterminate moments they do not count.
The ripple has passed, and the flash.
They listen to the tunneled breath of lungs,
And sense somewhere deep in earth's crust
A groan.

Did you hear that? she asks.

Waiting for Life

In Imbabwa, south from the outskirts
Of Cairo, a young woman steals her arm out the window,
Feeling for rain. Her husband, the fastidious American
Doctor, visits the city every Thursday, and from her perch
On the sill she may glimpse his return.
Slender white arm snakes above the dust in search of rain.
Next year perhaps they will start a family, but now
In the drought she seeks only to lift water to her lips,
Lift water, comb rain through her hair. She considers
Dinner, out she believes, with friends: how
Flat her stomach will look in the ivory silk
That she has set aside for the evening.

Dedication

If I had put the same energy
I spent grieving you
Into loving you,
I'd long since have found you.
Ahh.

The Pantomime Horse

*...two people pretending humorously to be
a horse by dressing in special clothes and standing
one behind the other...*   Cambridge Dictionary

Years of practice, halves hewn to one flesh,
years of rear hoof nicking the lag leg ahead,
oopses and sorrys. A comic ballet
of bagged-head beginners. Tokens mark the years:
leather for the third, linen for the twelfth.
But leather splits and linen pills. The chip
grows durable: sapphire at thirty-five,
diamond at sixty. Eventually
(walk before you canter) they try the next gait,
But where its key? How to spring its latch?
Daft turns deft, tangles are parsed, creases smoothed.
Warn me when you turn. Telegraph when you stop.
And what if the wires are down?

The grafts outlast the oaths.
Synchrony sands down ineptitude,
and reveries of distant pastures dim.
Rehearsing they alternate, switch fore and aft,
fuse first by words, then habit, then being,
catching the other's totter, counterweighting.
Crises of direction, speed, parturition,
even identity, solve –perhaps resolve,
dissolve–themselves. In easy optimism
each assumes the other's good knees,

firm hocks, limbs. From two wills
one voice, one act.

Every producer knows, duos
are twice the risk. And sure as Time,
the sharpest stress finds the weakest bone.

Death and Dying

Death smiles at us all, all we can do is smile back.
—Marcus Aurelius

Estragon: I can't go on like this.
Vladimir: That's what you think.
—Samuel Beckett, Waiting for Godot

Summiting

To age is to ascend a steep cone,
A helical climb where each circuit
Is shorter than the last, until
A step with your right foot
Trips your left heel, upraised.
Ah, that's the point.

To an Old Man Dying

(for Lucien)

"I'm coming back as a sea lion," he said,
"To traverse the seven seas.
I'll swim from Norway to the Coast of Japan,
Or not, whichever I please."

"But how will I know you?" she asked, distressed.
"All sea lions look alike."
"I'll wear a gold candle that burns on my head,
And eye-glitter green as a pike."

"I'm coming back as a lichen," he said,
"To cling to an oak's northern side.
I'll contemplate life without saying a word,
And day after day abide."

"I'm coming back as an osprey," he said.
"I've hit on my ultimate wish.
Where all there's to do is hang on the wind,
And fly and fuck and fish."

"If you come back as a lichen," she said,
"I'll know which blossom is you.
I'll scrape you screaming off the soggy bark
And boil you in my stew."

"If I find you've returned as some ear-piercing bird,
I'll get out my trusty bow,
And the first time you soar past, you son of a bitch,
An arrow will bring you low."

"For easing the hurt," and she grabbed his lapel,
"The choices have boiled down to two.
Either come back as me with a hole in my gut,
Or simply come back as you."

Exit

Leaving Bad, the Frontier town,
You pass the sign post,
"To Worse 3 mi."
No other road, no other sign.

Lines in Elegy

In every silence sits a stone,
A pit in every peach.
In every heart a hollow place
That solace cannot reach.
In every cloud a bud of blood,
In every pleasure rue,
And each tomorrow brings a trace
Of what I lost with you.

The Ballad of Willy Loman

They say that us salesmen are at a dead end,
But not me. Guaranty, I'm the customer's friend.
My territory's dotted with people who care,
Who treat me gracious, who treat me square.
They know my car —Pontiac Catalina,
Two-tone hard-top, green and greener.
When I drive up with my order book
I'm greeted respectful, a shake and a look.
Deedily doo deedily dun, the deed the deed, deed'll be done.

That's what I sing-song as I clock the miles,
And clock the rejections and clock the smiles.
The territory's endless, it cannot be covered—
Big as an Empire, a state to be suffered,
And every hotel room is like the last,
And every closed door where you haven't been asked,
And in every empty a bare bulb for the room—
And a pint of rye whiskey to chase off the gloom.

Still there's a part you never can chase,
Some gut dwelling part where you can't close the space.
In a half-inch of dust on the Pontiac's fender.
I write it all out then go on a bender
That uses up twice my weekly per diems.
And so to kill time, I hang out at museums,
At leatherette diners with free saltines.
Order book empty, soul in smithereens.

I know I'd be gold if I just got to Corning,
Just one more stop on a Thursday morning
And after that, the honey pot—I kill in Corning.
Geneva is tough, local competition.
I die in Geneva, it's a lose-lose mission,
But the route's the route, you follow the route,
No slacking, no cutting, no turning about.
I'm stopped at the front desk, You phone for a space?
Go wait in the lobby, don't you know your place?
Hell I've called on them since she was in diapers
But I drag my ass out, those cheap Swedish vipers,
You're in deep trouble when the customer's Swede,
If they cut themselves shaving, they're too cheap to bleed.

Get out, drive hell-bent through the October morning
'Cause I know I'll be gold once I get to Corning.
God help me in Corning but I get short shrift,
Goose-egged, garnicht, on the schneid, stiffed.
They've placed their order, just arrived by rail,
Saves the commission, just ordered by mail.
Saves you the trouble, Willy, easier this way,
You won't mind, Willy, ought to make your day.
Hours from Geneva, twice that from home,
Back to the hotel, dinner alone.
Deed'll he do, giddly gun, the deed indeed, it'll be done.

Willy or won't he, and where, how, and when?
A bold act: the boys will respect me again,
And again my wife think me the pitch-perfect mate
Who runs all the errands, who never works late,
Who weed-kills the lawn and prunes the dead roses,
Performs a full line-up of wax-paper poses.
Whose eyes are all dotted, whose lists are all crossed,
Who'll reach home exhausted in need of exhaust.
Deed'll doo, deed'll dun, the deed indeed, deed'll be
done.

Armageddon in Suburbia

Tiffany eloped with an immigrant Gambian
And Father collapsed —a coronary spasm.
Our grieving Lexus o-d'd on Ambien,
And the Porsche SUV drove into a chasm.

Emma and Amelia are working the street,
Rains have ruined the coffee-table book,
Fentanyl took Lucas off his feet,
And lava is filling the breakfast nook.

When Bel Aire disappeared in the Andreas fault
Sheila had run off with a dopplegang Barbie.
Trevor locked himself in the bomb-proof vault
With a liter of Grey Goose and the NYRB.

The threats of Revelation are coming to life:
Junior, when he missed the winning free throw,
Married a trans chap with two kids and wife.
We're pitching a treatment to a major studio.

Q. E. D.

Death is markedly different from life
but not without traits to commend it.
No word for pain, cravenness, hate,
nor any need.
I could go on indefinitely,
but you can't.
See what I mean?

November Sun

Bleak and saddest of times
As light leaks from the southern sky
And losing heart color fades from the eye;
Then flees. The sun, a distant and cool star.
Leaves lie in the gutters, random trash
Discarded by some negligent titan.
Swept when snows melt and skies lighten
You cannot blame it on the planet's orbit:

Nearing the sun, boreal earth prolongs night,
Then bends away, as might a dinner guest
From a wearisome partner, as if unable
To bear the tedium. She leans and sighs,
Hoping for coffee to be served so
She may once again turn the table.

Fragment

I shake her by the shoulders
A lover's prod, and her eyelids shiver.
Again, so the years begin to tumble from her hair
Motes of dust from the imaginary mortar
That cements memory to her.
It is not youth I want to recover but
The wealth that youth had.
Spilling its coins on the cobbles,
Beyond reclaim
I want to shake the past from her, shake it so
I can scoop it up and together
We can spend it.

Numina

Listening to Coltrane
assures me that
any world to come–
forget the pitchforks and chains,
burbling sulfur, smarmy harps–
will have music –forget the
ethos, gods, traffic signals,
humans –I don't grasp.

The Agnostic

He doesn't believe in an afterlife,
No matter whose preacher rants and shouts.
No Heavenly unguents or mawkish saints,
No mephitic Hell with pitchforks and restraints.
He doesn't believe in an afterlife,
And as to this one, he has his doubts.

The Widower

Afterwards he lost his appetite.
When two blue quail flushed from the thatch
As he crossed the fresh-hayed field, his eyes
No longer tracked their frenzied rush.
The dog froze, muzzle aimed, puzzled
That no shot followed. What had happened?
On he walked, no weight of weapon
Nudging the crook of his arm,
Yet another sensation that death
Had pilfered from him.

The Girls on the Boardwalk

Breath-stealing girls in white cotton prints.
Delphiniums and zinnia,
Bluebells on linen, bluebells on chintz—
Or are those delphinia?

Their bodies jointless, floating and lithe,
Their chatter beyond comprehension.
Daydreams don't stop them, they patter by, blithe
Intending no condescension.

I bisect their path, the ever-scheming man,
A posture of purpose, but risible.
They're blind to motive, my doddery plan,
For to them, you see, I'm invisible.

Pushing sea-air like dolphin, they smell only of youth,
And salt spray and breezes and lotion,
While I, of sulfur that age swaps for truth,
A sulfur of long-stale emotion.

The bargain's a cliché, one made with my fate,
I ponder with audible sigh,
As liquors from their perfume evaporate,
And the girls on the boards pass me by.

Strawman

Spineless, from hobo hat
to flagging soles, my disgust disguised,
stand I, the Strawman,
brainless and empty-eyed.

The fields: given over
to parked cars. Even the crows,
once mobbing, murdering,
have tired of my stock, comic pose.

I abide in circle center,
abandoned, alone, apart,
in rummaged vest, burlap, twine,
lacking, too, a heart.

Fearing electric Spring, Yule candles,
for my soul has dried to kindling.
See how chaff falls from hollow cuffs
as this rag body is dwindling

while the surround of trees
changes flags, grows moss.
Is it solitude, fear, or desuetude
that nails me to my cross?

My Obituary (in full)

Unless resurrected,
slighter than expected.

Transfiguration

A seam 'twixt
Dawn and light,
There and here,
Time and space,
Yawns,
The width of a thought.
So the minnow
That is life slips through,
Upstream
Towards the seedling star.

Making Art

To be a poet is a condition rather than a profession.
—Robert Graves

We make out of the quarrel with others, rhetoric,
but of the quarrel with ourselves, poetry.
—William Butler Yeats

Night Pilot

The tug of something live (Fish on the line!)
Tells him the kite remains aloft.
Blind fingers rely on the angle of twine.
Evening's inconstant breeze goes slack, and oft
Times he feels it plunging in the calm.
To earth indifferent, not connected,
Tied to heaven by a wire across his palm
He flies his craft without proof, undetected.
Now squints to see the starlight blotted out.
Across the skylake swims his skittling otter,
A hole in the heavens, stars put to rout.
By day he traces poems in water.

Zodiac

Dusk. In the last cuticle of sun,
They spark their wood, bring forth skin bags.
Remove the bones each has cached–
Tarsal of deer, carpal of dog,
Mandible of rat, humerus of dove–
And, metonymy of life itself,
The distal fingertip of an enemy.

Toss bones in the dirt, render them aloud.
The fires brighten. The villagers form
Rings around one roller of runes
Who tells their story over and again.
Dark deepens. Leather-skinned, the color of bark,
She kneels on crippled knees marked
On their caps where Goat-man
Has tattooed sap to ease the pain.

Without slate, papyrus, ink,
Without history or library, she
Climbs the hill to study the night.
The first poet, there she wrings stories
From stars. Of gods and killing seas,
Of a hive sings honey sweet,
Of thunder and crabs that crawl ashore
To steal babes from their straw.

Wrings out stories in the cadence of dust,
Of clouds, of winds, all wrought
From random, scattered points of light.
The villagers lie, faces upward, squinting
At the flint-struck sky, and listen silently.
She sees shapes where none exist,
And spins pinholes about our hill,
She is believed.

Genesis

Scripture fails to mention
The creation of human expressions.
Which did God choose first?
The smile when She saw
Her beasts of the air take flight?
The shock of the stricken Adam
The frown when the emigrees left Eden?
My money's on the smirk.

Sonnet Sixty-five

God's constant tricks reveal a prankster's taste
For farce. She fits us with the tools to love,
Paper, language, inks and wit—a waste
Of effort. Spoken words seem durable, sort of.
And those who put their ardor down in paint,
Sized canvas, pigmented oils, shellac,
Yet see their deepest colors grow faint;
Their warmest flesh, their dearest portraits crack.
Arthritis seats the dance, short breath the flute.
In time all verse goes dog-eared, creased and foxed,
Thalia's jokes grow stale, no longer suit,
Like blueprints for Parnassus, stored and boxed.
Even the sculptor, trusting the strength of bronze,
Recasts: Art and Eternity, two of Her cons.

Alcatraz

There are poems, the text said,
Imprisoned in every blank sheet.
I tried –lemon juice, the guano
Of starlings, warming the page
Over a candle's flame–
To incite a jailbreak.
All to no avail.

Bonnard

Vestal, she steals through the parted door on toes,
Winces at the chill of the brick, the chill of dark.
Within, the tub fills a hand's width from lip,
The water smokes with welcome, vague verdigris
Against porcelain walls. He has searched to find
The whites he wants —not washed or iridescent
To outshine the phosphorescence of her skin,
Antique white, blushed with a daub of honey.
He, now I, stare as she sheds her peignoir,
Skin pulsing, breath held, lifts a knee to the rim,
Leans to test the trembling water. It responds,
Ripples as a cat shrugs its spine to touch.
Close observation and a minimum of paint,
He murmurs, his eye and I alone with her.

Chekhov

She says this,
They say that,
He stands, leaves.
She mentions it.
He returns.
They have tea.

Bach

An ageless world covers, shadows our own.
Here, bones yield to ash, mountains to gravel,
Nothing lasts. But there! How to travel?
Watch children at play, catch the seashell's moan.

In the cathedral of music hear cosmic sounds of spheres.
Walk the path that he laid by fugal weaves
To enter a world a Buddha might conceive.
Is it possible that the path runs through the ears?

Metaphysics emerge from variations on a theme.
Each canon, quaver, descant spans the divide,
Crosses from transience and all that dies or died,
To a fixéd realm, where our worth the notes redeem.

Who could imagine that escape from all dimension
Lay coiled in the braid of a two-part invention?

Smith Corona

I write in silence,
Wistful for the slap of keys on paper—
A tattoo, if not of progress, then industry—
The bell, E-flat, music welcome as
The snap of the finish line.
The staccato roll of the platen
As I pull out a page,
Soiled evidence of time misspent.

A Light Supper

To complete the day, he pens
A poem that pops in the mouth
With sweet and plenary fullness.
A grape that bursts against
The tongue and satisfies
His cravings.
That singular grape,
Taken with a sip of water,
On which Cyrano dined.

Tweeting with Didi and Gogo

I've not done this before. Are you getting this?

    I don't quite know yet.

Well you must be if you're answering.

    I'm not answering, I'm saying I don't quite know.

You either know or don't know. It's binary.

    Winery? Did you mean winery?

Why in the world would I say WINERY.

    It must be the auto correct.

I don't understand.

    I guess I'm not getting it.

There's nothing to be done. Let's move on.

    Didn't you say we're limited as to characters?

That's right. 140 characters.

    But we've exceeded that.

140 characters per message, but unlimited messages.

    Unlimited?

Depending on your plan.

    I have no plan.

Your contract. Your contract with your carrier.

    I don't have a carrier. I don't even have a cat.

You're being difficult.

    How else should one be?

What do you mean?

    Being. I find it difficult.

We are simply exchanging tweets. Nothing more.

    And nothing less?

And nothing less. Keep that in mind. You seem forgetful.

I don't seem. Therefore I am forgetful.

What is it you're forgetting?

I wouldn't remember, would I?

I suppose not.

Do you object to forgetting?

What's to object?

Forgetting seems like death, don't you think?

Quite alike.

Are they the same?

No. In death there is no growth. No love. No whisky.

Is there a God?

It doesn't say here.

Where?

In the script.

I didn't know there was a script.

What do you think? Is there a God?

If there were a God there would be whisky.

And if there's whisky?

Then it wouldn't matter about God.

Do you suppose?

Not often.

It's an odd word, 'suppose'. It sounds like a brand of stocking.

But there is no other pose. We're allowed only the one.

Not true. There is impose and expose.

Why do you suppose?

It must be human nature.

What does it mean?

Nature? What's outside: rocks, trees, worm droppings.

    No, no, I mean the word.

The word was in the beginning.

    The word "suppose".

Oh.. From the Latin, <u>ponere</u>, to place. And <u>sub</u>, under.

    To place under?

Correct.

    Then, were I buried, would I not be <u>supposed</u> to be under the earth.

But you will be.

    I will be what?

You will be supposed to be under the earth. And you will be.

    Well. That's all right, then.

It is.

    There's nothing to be done.

Isn't this where we came in?

The Rings of Saturn

Look aslant with a child's eye at a faint star,
Then slowly focus and it disappears.
This is physiology, not magic:
Cells that sense light bunch at the retina's fringe.
Now attend the simplest, two-part Bach fugue;
Separate the triads. My ear finds the third,
But look at the score: I put it in.
Bach has enlisted me in the performance,
No contract, no tux. Zilch
False completions fill our universe,
Connecting dots, drawing lines that aren't there:
Mirage, simulacra, myths, many –permanence, glory,
Go along to get along– are cozy as a warm bath.
Saturn's rings are no more than particles:
Ice, basal rock, sidereal sand,
Grains a micron long, gaps wide as Madagascar.
What lesson suits this uneven tale?
I bind the rings together. The beholder holds.

Three A. M.

I hear in night's hollow a tone—
The A-flat above middle C.
It lasts seconds, pauses, repeats.
I first think, This is getting old.
Then I realize: in a new galaxy
They're playing a concerto, and
Where I hear silence
Are melodies beyond my ken.

Ithaka

The poet told him it was the journey.
But, with the bus ride now
in its seventh hour
—he seats without springs,
the baby unchanged,
the food garlicked and stale—
he has his doubts.

Shades

Walk among them.
Softly, lest they scatter.
Dark-eyed juncos, hesitant,
Feed on fallen seed.

Feeding voles flee
At noises imagined.
Walk among them, Take notice
When the light is right,

Moments after glow,
That last wine-bodied burst,
Footfalls sound no scent of dust,
Only then they appear
When the light is right.

Stalk your agèd friend,
Pull at his jacket sleeve,
Give a gentle, weightless tug.
Unaware, caught off guard,
He disregards,
For the moment.

The Barge

A little girl with russet hair
Once whispered in my ear:
"I will not eat an unpeeled pear
Or sprouts or ginger beer."
To keep her news she made me swear,
And lock my lips in mime
And I have kept that secret close
Until this very time.

I carry many hidden thoughts
Of similar import,
A chap who envies astronauts,
A lad who hated sport,
A friend who took a Hershey bar
And left but never paid,
Another who confessed he loved
A Hilton hotel maid.

To cobblers, folks bring worn-out soles,
To bookmakers their bets,
To me they bring their crippled hopes,
New freight and old regrets.
They view their blemishes as large
And park them here with me
To stow them in a poem, this barge,
And tow it out to sea.

ABOUT THE AUTHOR

Bruce Ducker is the prize-winning author of eight novels and a book of short fictions. He has over 100 poems and stories in the nation's leading literary journals, including The New Republic; the Yale, Southern, Sewanee, Literary, and Hudson Reviews, and Poetry Magazine. A jazz pianist, he's also written the book, music and lyrics for three musical comedies. Born in New York City, he lives in Colorado.

ABOUT THE KINGSTON UNIVERSITY PRESS

Kingston University Press has been publishing high-quality commercial and academic titles since 2009. Our list has always reflected the diverse nature of the student and academic bodies at the university in ways that are designed to impact on debate, to hear new voices, to generate mutual understanding and to complement the values to which the university is committed.

While keeping true to our original mission, and maintaining our wide-ranging backlist titles, our most recent publishing focuses on bringing to the fore voices past and present that reflect and appeal to our community at the university as well as the wider reading community of readers and writers in Kingston, the UK and beyond.

As well as publishing the work of writers and poets from the university's vibrant writing community, we also partner with other disciplines around the university, and organisations from our local community, to bring their content to a wider readership.

Our books are all edited, designed and produced by postgraduate students at Kingston University, whose creativity and publishing skills bring the projects to life.

Follow us on Instagram @kingstonuniversitypress

Find out more about Kingston's postgraduate courses in Publishing and Creative Writing at www.kingston.ac.uk.

Milton Keynes UK
Ingram Content Group UK Ltd.
UKHW010821220424
441551UK00005B/385

9 781909 362789